DIGGING UP
the Past

Stonehenge

Essential Library

An Imprint of Abdo Publishing | www.abdopublishing.com

Stonehenge

BY MICHAEL CAPEK

CONTENT CONSULTANT
DR. T. L. THURSTON, PROFESSOR,
DEPT. OF ANTHROPOLOGY, UNIVERSITY AT BUFFALO
STATE UNIVERSITY OF NEW YORK

www.abdopublishing.com

Published by Abdo Publishing, a division of ABDO, PO Box 398166, Minneapolis, Minnesota 55439. Copyright © 2015 by Abdo Consulting Group, Inc. International copyrights reserved in all countries. No part of this book may be reproduced in any form without written permission from the publisher. Essential Library™ is a trademark and logo of Abdo Publishing.

Printed in the United States of America, North Mankato, Minnesota
032014
092014

Cover Photo: Simon Gurney/Thinkstock
Interior Photos: Simon Gurney/Thinkstock, 2; Thinkstock, 6, 19, 27, 97; Red Line Editorial, 8, 23; Corbis, 12, 39; North Wind/North Wind Picture Archives, 15; William Stukeley, 21; Photos.com/Thinkstock, 24, 35; Historical Picture Archive/Corbis, 30; Hulton Archive/Getty Images, 32; Lefteris Pitarakis/AP Images, 41; Chris Hellier/Corbis, 42; De Agostini/Getty Images, 46–47; Hulton-Deutsch Collection/Corbis, 49; Bettmann/Corbis, 50, 57; Chinch Gryniewicz/Ecoscene/CORBIS/Glow Images, 55; Dorling Kindersley RF/Thinkstock, 58–59; English Heritage/Arcaid/Corbis, 63; R J C Atkinson/English Heritage/Arcaid/Corbis, 64; Mary Evans Picture Library/Alamy, 70; Alastair Grant/AP Images, 75; iStock/Thinkstock, 76; Barry Batchelor/AP Images, 80; Kirsty Wigglesworth/AP Images, 84; Kazuhiko Sano/National Geographic Creative, 87; Julian Elliott/Shutterstock Images, 89; Adam Stanford/Aerial-Cam for National Geographic/AP Images, 92

Editor: Lauren Coss
Series Designer: Becky Daum

Library of Congress Control Number: 2014932251

Cataloging-in-Publication Data

Capek, Michael.
 Stonehenge / Michael Capek.
   p. cm. -- (Digging up the past)
Includes bibliographical references and index.
ISBN 978-1-62403-237-0
1. Stonehenge (England)--Juvenile literature.   2. Wiltshire (England)--Antiquities--Juvenile literature.   3. Megalithic monuments--England--Wiltshire--Juvenile literature.   I. Title.
936.2--dc23

                                                2014932251

CONTENTS

CHAPTER 1   If Stones Could Talk   6

CHAPTER 2   The Antiquarians   12

CHAPTER 3   Searching for a Pattern   24

CHAPTER 4   The Victorians   32

CHAPTER 5   Protecting the Stones   42

CHAPTER 6   More Discoveries   50

CHAPTER 7   Stonehenge Decoded?   64

CHAPTER 8   Stonehenge for All   76

CHAPTER 9   The Riverside Project   84

TIMELINE   98

DIGGING UP THE FACTS   100

GLOSSARY   102

ADDITIONAL RESOURCES   104

SOURCE NOTES   106

INDEX   110

ABOUT THE AUTHOR   112

1

If Stones Could Talk

Nobody discovered Stonehenge, at least not in the way Machu Picchu, the tomb of King Tut, or other archaeological wonders were discovered. Stonehenge has been in plain sight in south-central England for thousands of years. However, until the early 1900s, no one knew who had built Stonehenge, how they had built it, or why.

Stonehenge is a mysterious stone circle that lies on southern England's Salisbury Plain.

WHERE IS STONEHENGE?

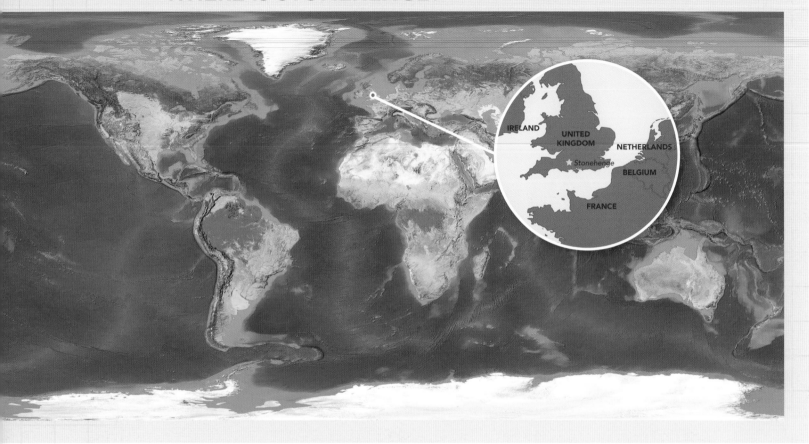

WHAT IS STONEHENGE?

Stonehenge is an ancient stone circle that stands on a hill in the middle of Salisbury Plain. This 300-square-mile (777 sq km) grassland is near the River Avon in the county of Wiltshire, England, 80 miles (129 km) west of London,

England.[1] There are many stone circles across England, but Stonehenge is one of the largest and most famous. Archaeologists now believe the oldest part of the circle was built more than 5,000 years ago.

The name *Stonehenge* comes from Saxon words that mean "hanging stones." To modern archaeologists, however, the term *henge* simply refers to an ancient, circular earthwork, with or without standing stones, that has a ditch on the inside of a bank surrounding a flat, central area.

The henge at Stonehenge is approximately 330 feet (100 m) in diameter and has a bank of piled-up soil that once was probably six feet (1.8 m) high.[2] Today, after thousands of years of erosion, the henge is barely visible beneath the grass. Just inside the henge is a ring of 56 steep-sided holes, known as Aubrey Holes. A long earthwork called the Avenue extends outward from Stonehenge's entrance for more than two miles (3.2 km) until it ends at the River Avon. The Avenue is a pathway approximately 70 feet (21 m) wide

STONE CARPENTERS

Stonehenge's lintels are held in place by a system of mortise-and-tenon and tongue-and-groove joinery. This is a method wood carpenters used for centuries. They cut a knob or pin at the top or end of a piece of wood that fits snugly into a hole drilled into another piece. This creates a joint that is not easily separated. No one has ever seen another stone structure from ancient times built in this way. Archaeologists believe this may suggest Stonehenge was designed to be a stone representation of a wooden building.

that ancient workers carefully leveled and marked with parallel ditches on each side.[3]

INSIDE STONEHENGE

Stonehenge's most noticeable feature is the ruined circle of hand-shaped sarsen stones. These sandstone rocks litter the southern English countryside. Most of the sarsen stones at Stonehenge show evidence of being artificially shaped to have a relatively uniform appearance. Stonehenge has 30 upright stones arranged in a circle approximately 100 feet (30 m) in diameter.[4] Curved lintels, or stone cross pieces, rest horizontally across the top of the upright stones.

A group of stones called bluestones once stood just inside the sarsen stones in a circle approximately 75 feet (23 m) in diameter. Archaeologists believe approximately 60 of these stones once stood in a ring spaced only a few feet apart from one another. Only six stones remain upright now. Others lay flat or broken on the ground.

Inside this bluestone circle stands a group of five sarsen trilithons, each made up of two stones topped by a lintel. The trilithons are arranged in a horseshoe shape approximately 45 feet (14 m) across. The shortest trilithons are approximately 20 feet (6.1 m) and the tallest is more than 24 feet (7.3 m) tall.[5] Only three trilithons still have lintels. Inside the trilithon horseshoe, archaeologists have found evidence of a second horseshoe of smaller stones. At one time, 19 bluestones made up this horseshoe. Today only six of these stones remain.

More than half of the original stone structure is missing. Some of the fallen stones lie broken and half-buried where they toppled long ago. Other stones have simply disappeared.

MORE STONES

Other features of Stonehenge include a large sandstone slab known as the Altar Stone. In the 1700s and 1800s, archaeologists imagined it might have been used as an altar. The Altar Stone is approximately 16 feet (4.9 m) long.[6] It once stood upright, but it now lies under other fallen pieces of stone. On the northeast side of Stonehenge is a gap that served as an entrance.

Just inside this entrance is a 21-foot- (6.4 m) tall stone known as the Slaughter Stone.[7] In the 1700s and 1800s, archaeologists imagined it might have been used for human sacrifices. Recent archaeological excavations, however, have suggested it was actually once part of a gateway trilithon at the entrance that fell over and broke.

What remains, though, reveals the incredible level of workmanship and physical effort that went into building Stonehenge. What archaeologists have learned about the structure that remains has given new insight into ancient humans. It has taught us Neolithic society was much more complex and advanced than many people ever imagined.

The Antiquarians

One of the first written mentions of Stonehenge was in a book written by Henry of Huntingdon, an early church official, in 1130 CE. Henry's book, *Historia Anglorum* (The History of the English People), discusses English history, including various wonders and oddities. Among these, Henry lists *Stanenges*, great hinged or hanging stones. At this remarkable place, Henry wrote,

Since ancient times, Stonehenge has fascinated and puzzled people living in England.

Stones of wonderful size have been erected after the manner of doorways, so that doorway appears to have been raised upon doorway; and no one can conceive how such great stones have been so raised aloft, or why they were built there.[1]

Archaeologists believe Henry was talking about Stonehenge.

In 1136 CE, another church official, Geoffrey of Monmouth, attempted to explain how the stones got to Salisbury. In *The History of the Kings of Britain*, Geoffrey told the story of Aurelius Ambrosius, a king of England from the 400s CE, who won a spectacular victory in a battle against his Saxon enemies. Ambrosius was so pleased, he decided to build a monument as a memorial to the victory. According to Geoffrey, Merlin the Magician used a magical machine to move huge stones from a stone circle in Ireland to Salisbury Plain. Once there, Merlin rebuilt the stone circle. What Merlin accomplished was a miracle, Geoffrey concluded, but really only proved that "artistry was worth more than any brute strength."[2]

That story, with minor variations, became the most popular and frequently retold history of Stonehenge for the next 600 years. Many other theories surfaced about how Stonehenge came to be, but none of them were as easy to believe or understand as Merlin's magic. Most people felt normal human beings could not have built anything as massive as Stonehenge.

DIGGING WITH A PURPOSE

One of the earliest excavations to see what was beneath Stonehenge took place in 1620. The Duke of Buckingham, a friend of England's King James I, went to Stonehenge and ordered servants to dig a deep pit in the middle. He hoped to find interesting relics, or maybe gold, which would please the king. But Buckingham found only animal bones and charcoal.

After the Duke of Buckingham's dig, King James I asked architect Inigo Jones to conduct his own investigation of Stonehenge. Jones was the most noted architect of his time. He had

In English legends, Merlin was a powerful magician who served in the courts of King Arthur and his father.

studied architecture all over the world and recognized that Stonehenge was unique. After investigating the site, Jones decided an architectural genius from ancient Rome must have come to England and designed the structure. Jones was certain the monument could not have been built by the native Britons of ancient times.

Medical doctor Walter Charlton disagreed with Jones's theory. In the mid-1600s, Charlton examined Stonehenge himself. In 1663, he published a book stating his theory about the site's origins. Charlton determined Danish Viking invaders had erected the stones long ago as a place to crown their kings. There was little evidence for this theory, however, and very few people agreed with it.

AUBREY'S THEORY

In the 1660s, another explorer came to examine Stonehenge, but with better results. John Aubrey was a wealthy writer and collector of local folklore. Like many upper-class gentlemen of the 1600s, he was fascinated by old things and referred to himself as an antiquarian. These were typically educated, curious men who had the time and money to study history and search for artifacts.

Aubrey traveled all over Wiltshire and the nearby area, looking at henges and stone circles and making detailed notes and drawings. He had a keen mind and a burning desire to understand who had built these places and why. He knew the old stories about Stonehenge, too, and that other antiquarians before him had studied Stonehenge.

Aubrey did not agree with the theories put forth by Jones and Charlton. He set out to do his own investigation. In 1649, Aubrey had discovered a stone circle at Avebury, approximately 20 miles (32 km) north of Stonehenge that no one had noticed in modern times. Aubrey decided the best way to understand Stonehenge was to compare it with other ancient circles in the area. Avebury, Stonehenge, and other circles throughout England, Scotland, Wales, and Ireland all appeared to be related to one another.

Aubrey understood the stone circles were ancient. He knew they were far too old to have been built by Vikings, who had been active in England between 800 and 1100 CE. Many of the circles were in places no Romans had traveled. Therefore, Aubrey concluded, ancient Britons must have built

THE CIRCLE AT AVEBURY

Aubrey discovered the Avebury henge in 1649, and he could hardly believe no one had noticed it since ancient times. The circle is enormous. In fact, much of the English village of Avebury lies inside the henge. It is the largest stone circle in the world. The circle covers more than 28 acres (11.3 ha).[4] Approximately 130 Stonehenges could fit inside Avebury's outer circle. The circle once contained more than 600 standing stones, but only 75 stones can be seen today.

all of these sites, including Stonehenge. He believed the circles had been temples for ancient Celtic priests known as Druids.

Aubrey's book *Monumenta Britannica* describes his careful methods of research. He made detailed drawings of Stonehenge. He taught himself to use surveying instruments to make precise measurements. He looked for similarities in objects and sites and classified them. In this way, he was able to draw logical conclusions and back them up with proof. Because he was the first to use scientific methods that would later become the basis of modern archaeological research, Aubrey is often viewed as the first true English archaeologist.

STUKELEY'S DISCOVERIES

Aubrey's techniques influenced doctor and antiquarian William Stukeley in the 1700s. Stukeley made diagrams

The stone circle at Avebury is the largest in the world.

and discoveries that went far beyond Aubrey's careful observations. One of these discoveries was the Avenue, which he traced from Stonehenge, past the Heel Stone, a large stone standing outside Stonehenge's entrance, toward the River Avon. Stukeley noted that the monument's axis, which follows the Avenue, seemed to align with the rising midsummer sunrise. Stukeley also discovered a strange earthwork near Stonehenge. He thought the 350-foot- (107 m) wide, two-mile- (3.2 km) long feature looked like a chariot track, so he called it the *Cursus*, which is Latin for "racetrack."[5]

Between 1721 and 1724, Stukeley did an extensive survey of the area around Stonehenge. He excavated inside the stone circle and at nearby burial mounds,

DRUIDS

Exactly who and what historical Druids were is still debated today. Druidic ceremonies were secret, and nothing they taught or did was ever written down. According to most archaeologists, Druids were religious leaders of the Celts, people who came to England in approximately 600 BCE. When Romans invaded England in the 40s CE, the Druids resisted Roman ways and convinced others to do the same. As a result, Roman soldiers made Druids a prime target. Thousands of Druids were killed in battles or surprise raids by Roman troops. Most modern archaeologists believe Druids did not build Stonehenge, and it is unlikely they used the site as a temple.

DR. WILLIAM STUKELEY

A friend of scientists Isaac Newton and Edmund Halley, Stukeley was fascinated by Stonehenge and studied every aspect of the structure from approximately 1719 to his death in 1765. Stukeley was a superior artist with a physician's eye for detail. In middle age, he abandoned medicine and archaeology and became a country parson. He finally published his Stonehenge notes and drawings in 1740, but the book was very different from what it had started out to be. Later in life, Stukeley became obsessed with Druids. He associated them with every aspect of Stonehenge, even though doing so was historically inaccurate. He helped make Druids part of English popular culture, but he ruined the chances that his work would ever be taken seriously.

Stukeley's obsession with Druids, shown in one of his drawings, discredited much of his later work.

A STONE OBSERVATORY?

Stukeley's discovery that Stonehenge's axis is almost perfectly aligned with the rising midsummer sun created an idea that is still debated today. Many people believe Stonehenge was designed and built to be a massive stone observatory. Over the centuries, people have proposed many different theories surrounding this idea.

Some believed Stonehenge was used for tracking the movements of stars and planets. Others thought people once used the stone circle to predict lunar and solar eclipses. Not until the 1900s, however, would knowledge and technology advance far enough for people to actually be able to explore these alignments scientifically.

called barrows. Many people had previously believed these barrows served as mass graves for fallen warriors. Stukeley's digs convinced him the barrows featured single burials of important men and women. He believed some of these were native Britons who had built Stonehenge, probably around 460 BCE. Stukeley arrived at this date based on measurements he made with his compass and his knowledge that the earth's magnetic field, and therefore the direction of due north, shifts in a regular cycle over the centuries. This complicated calculation marked the first time a scientific instrument was used to make an educated guess about Stonehenge's age.

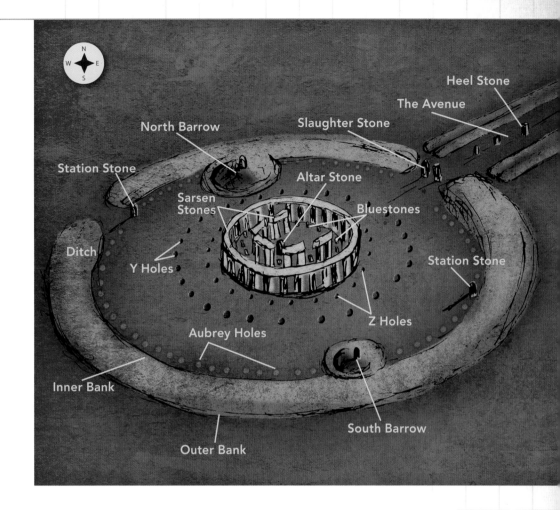

Today William Stukeley is recognized as a pioneer of modern archaeology. His precise measurement of Stonehenge, his incredibly accurate drawings, and, like Aubrey, his ability to see connections and similarities between many different sites and draw conclusions provided new insight into Stonehenge. His detailed records of the site, at a time when record keeping was not considered important, are invaluable to modern archaeologists.

3

Searching for a Pattern

After Aubrey and Stukeley, scientific investigation at Stonehenge lagged for decades. But as the 1700s drew to a close, an earthshaking event drew attention back to the stone circle once again.

In the 1800s, excavations at Stonehenge would yield new discoveries.

In 1797, farmers plowing a field near Stonehenge felt the ground shake. Soon after, someone passing near the stone circle noticed one of the inner sarsen trilithons had fallen. The topmost lintel had landed and rolled, striking another upright stone in the outer circle.

No one was particularly surprised. Other stones had obviously toppled before, and that group of three stones had been leaning for many years. However since it was the first such fall in recorded history, it was still noteworthy. It showed the stones were not immune to the forces of nature—particularly gravity.

The fall also revealed how shallowly that particular set of stones had been placed in the ground. Only approximately three feet (0.9 m) of the 22-foot- (6.7 m) tall stone had been underground.[1] It had been packed with dirt and pieces of rock to keep from toppling.

CUNNINGTON'S FIRST DIG

William Cunnington, a local wool merchant and antiquarian, soon arrived to examine the damage.

Poking around in the shallow hole left by the fallen stone, he unearthed some pottery pieces. He had found similar pieces in the many ancient barrows scattered around Salisbury Plain. The pottery looked to be Roman. But Cunnington felt certain Stonehenge was older than the Romans, who had controlled much of Great Britain from the 40s to the 400s CE. He hoped by digging up more evidence in and around Stonehenge, he might be able to find something that would help him solve the great mystery of who had erected the stones and when.

In 1802, Cunnington excavated at Stonehenge, unearthing some charred animal bones, pieces of deer antlers, and more pottery. However, these finds were also mixed with more

Roman ruins can still be found across England.

MIXING OF ARTIFACTS

The mixed layers may have had something to do with the fact that the Wiltshire countryside had been farmed for many years. Plows frequently turned up bones and relics, which were either reburied or tossed aside. For centuries, souvenir and treasure hunters had also rifled through Stonehenge and burial barrows looking for treasures. These amateur diggers may have removed and scattered objects. Rabbits and other burrowing animals did their share of mixing layers, too.

recent Roman pottery. He had better success digging near the Slaughter Stone, a large stone just inside Stonehenge's entrance. Cunnington dug into the chalky ground beneath the stone. He was excited to see the actual marks the builders' hammerstones had made on three sides. He suspected from this the stone had once stood upright.

PERFECT PARTNERS

Because of Cunnington's clever work at Stonehenge, Colt Hoare, another antiquarian, asked Cunnington to work for him as an excavator. Hoare was also hoping to find out who had built Stonehenge. The two men made a survey of all the ancient burials they could find in Wiltshire. In 1802, Cunnington and a small crew of workers began excavating them. By 1807, Cunnington had dug into more than 600 burial sites, including 200 near Stonehenge. But a great deal of what he had found was still confusing. At the time, most archaeologists used layers to arrive at approximate dates for artifacts. Older objects were buried deeper, and newer artifacts were shallower. However, the artifacts Cunnington found were almost always mixed. Pieces of very ancient pottery, stone tools, and more recent bronze and gold objects were often lying together.

By 1810, neither Hoare nor Cunnington was pleased with the progress their dig had made. They had a storehouse filled with relics but could draw no meaningful conclusions from them. Cunnington was particularly discouraged. He began to wonder if Stonehenge's builders were a people far older than anyone had previously suspected. Many of the barrows contained burials he recognized as being extremely old. However, he had no way of knowing or proving exactly how old they were.

THE THREE-AGE DIVISION OF PREHISTORY

The confusion and frustration of Hoare and Cunnington was in part due to their lack of understanding of prehistory. In approximately 1820, Danish archaeologist Christian Thomsen proposed a

WHERE ARE CUNNINGTON'S FINDS?

No one is certain what happened to the artifacts Hoare and Cunnington uncovered during their excavations. In fact, the whereabouts of almost every artifact collected from Stonehenge or the surrounding area before 1900 is unknown. Thousands of items that have provided knowledge and insight to modern archaeologists have simply vanished.

three-age division of prehistory. His study of European artifacts suggested there had been an early period of history before humankind discovered the art of metal craft. He called this period the Stone Age. Modern archaeologists believe the Stone Age likely ended in approximately 2500 BCE in England. Later, during a period Thomsen called the Bronze Age, people learned to make and use soft metal. In England, the Bronze Age likely lasted from approximately 2500 to 1000 BCE. Then came the Iron Age, in which humans learned to smelt harder, more durable metals. Thanks to Thomsen's eras, archaeologists finally had a way of classifying and understanding the things they found.

Stonehenge has held great meaning for people living in Great Britain throughout history.

4

The Victorians

In 1837, Queen Victoria ascended to the British throne. Her reign, from 1837 to 1901, is known as the Victorian era. This was a period of intense scientific advancement in Great Britain. New inventions from around the world, including the light bulb, internal combustion engine, sewing machine, elevator, telephone, movies, and many others, revolutionized the way people lived and worked. New ideas, such as naturalist Charles Darwin's theory of natural

By the mid-1800s, Stonehenge had become a popular tourist destination for wealthy British people.

DARWIN'S WORMS

Naturalist Charles Darwin was fascinated by earthworms. He observed the constant churning of billions of these creatures actually makes objects on the surface sink into the soil over time. In 1877, he found evidence of this near Stonehenge's sarsens. In fact, worms are probably responsible for at least some of the confusing mixture of relics from different eras at Stonehenge.

selection, challenged long-held views of human origins and changed the way people thought.

A NEW AGE, OLD IDEAS

When it came to Stonehenge, however, science did not make a great deal of progress. More was written about Stonehenge during the latter half of the 1800s than during any previous period. The problem was that most of the writings simply rehashed established ideas about who had built Stonehenge and when they did it.

Most people still believed Romans or the native English people they conquered must have laid the stones. Stukeley's Druids still haunted peoples' imaginations. Those few who believed Stonehenge was older still had no way of proving how old it truly was. Thomsen's proposal of a three-age division of prehistory had helped archaeologists classify different eras. However, they still had no way of determining exact dates for these eras. Most scientists held firm to the idea that any people who might have existed before the Bronze Age would have been far too primitive to build anything as elegant as Stonehenge.

Charles Darwin

The Victorian era did affect Stonehenge in other ways, though. Victorians visited Stonehenge in vast numbers. In fact, the stones became one of the most popular sites in England for picnics, day trips, and family outings. A direct railway line from London to Salisbury opened in 1857, making it even easier for tourists to visit the stones. A summer solstice fair was held on the grounds, with music, food, games, and entertainment. This attraction drew thousands from London and other cities to Salisbury Plain. Many tourists climbed on and carved their names into the sarsens and bluestones.

THE GUARDIANS

During the 1800s, various self-appointed guardians monitored Stonehenge. These were usually locals who took it upon themselves to greet visitors, tend to horses, and act as unofficial guides—for tips, of course. One guardian, William Judd of Mattington, made a living taking tourists' pictures.

He kept a ladder handy, which he rented to those who wished to stand atop the lintels. Unfortunately, the guardians did not do much to protect the stones. They even sold visitors small pieces of the stones if the price was right. Some visitors brought hammers to chip their own souvenirs.

Despite the floods of casual visitors, some serious scientific research still took place at Stonehenge during the 1800s. In 1865, John Lubbock, Lord Avebury, published *Prehistoric Times*, in which he presented a new view of the Stone Age. He saw major differences in the relics people classified as being from the Stone Age. Using this information, he divided the Stone Age into two divisions—early and late. He called the early division Paleolithic, an age when cave-dwelling people made and used crudely formed stone tools and weapons. The later division he called Neolithic. This was the age when humans began farming. Lubbock believed Stonehenge's builders had lived in the Neolithic period, but exactly when these periods had occurred was unclear to Victorians.

Representing the prevailing point of view, archaeologist Sir Daniel Wilson did not agree with Lubbock's view of Stonehenge. The site, he wrote, "is certainly not a work of the Stone Period, and probably not of the Bronze Period, with the exception of its little central circle."[1] Wilson held the view most people of this period had, that prehistoric people would not have been advanced enough to build anything close to as complex as Stonehenge.

Medical doctor John Thurnam attempted to apply forensic detective work to Stonehenge in the 1860s. Using Hoare's *Ancient Wiltshire* as his guide, he dug into the Salisbury barrows. Thurnam was looking for skulls. Cunnington and Hoare had removed many valuable items from the tombs, but they had left behind the skeletons. Thurnam had plenty of material to study.

Thurnam noted the barrows clustered around Stonehenge had different shapes. Some were long, while others were round. The long mounds contained almost no metal objects, so Thurnam reasoned they were likely Stone Age burials. The round barrows were full of bronze weapons and ornaments. These metal items suggested the round barrows were more recent, Bronze Age burials. Since round and long barrows were found in equal numbers near Stonehenge, Thurnam concluded that Stonehenge must have been a Bronze Age temple that had been built upon an older Stone Age site that had once been the burial place of Neolithic chiefs.

A MATHEMATICAL RECKONING

In the 1870s, English archaeologist Flinders Petrie approached Stonehenge's age from a completely different angle. He thought it might be possible to determine the age of a structure by measuring it and then mathematically determining what unit of length the builders had used. For instance, scholars knew Roman builders used a scale based on a unit that was 11.68 modern inches (29.67 cm) in length. The Phoenicians' measurements included a foot that was the equivalent of 22.51 modern inches (57.18 cm).[2] Stukeley had considered a similar idea years earlier. He had judged the Stonehenge masons had used a unit he called the Druid cubit, which was approximately 20.8 modern inches (52.83 cm).[3]

Petrie's measurements of Stonehenge brought him to the conclusion the builders had used two different scales of measurement. One scale unit for the stonework appeared to follow the Roman foot. Another scale unit was 224.8 modern inches (571 cm) long.[4] Petrie concluded Stonehenge was built in two phases. One happened before the Romans came to England in the 100s CE. Another part of Stonehenge was built later, after the Romans left, around 400 CE. Petrie believed the only way to make sure he had his measurements right was to dig out the stones and suspend them. But the owner of the land Stonehenge sat on refused to give Petrie permission for the risky maneuver.

Flinders Petrie was known for his explorations of Stonehenge and other ancient sites.

Instead, Petrie turned his attention to yet another Stonehenge puzzle. This one had to do with the stones' supposed astronomical alignments. Scientists had been fascinated with this idea ever since Stukeley had noted the Avenue and Heel Stone's apparent orientation toward the midsummer solstice sunrise. Petrie wanted to see if he could use this alignment to calculate how long ago Stonehenge had been built.

Petrie had raised an extremely complex question. His theory was based on the assumption that ancient people built and used Stonehenge as an astronomical observatory, which still had not been proven. Petrie's inquiry took into account the changing position of the sunrise over many centuries. By considering this variable, Petrie could calculate how long ago the sun

COUNTING STONES

A popular folktale from early times claims no one who counts the stones of Stonehenge ever arrives at the same number twice. Over the years, it became popular for visitors to count the stones and compare numbers, which never seemed to match. Some people thought Merlin's magic was responsible. The more practical explanation was that over the years the number *did* often change. People broke apart and carried away stones for souvenirs or for building projects.

would have actually risen directly over Stonehenge's Heel Stone. This calculation would give him the approximate year Stonehenge was built or was in common use. Petrie's mathematical formula produced a date of 730 CE.

MORE MATHEMATICS

No one seriously accepted Petrie's date. His points of reference inside Stonehenge were questionable, and there were too many variables in his math. The date he had arrived on was also far too recent to be accurate.

In 1901, Norman Lockyer, a noted astronomer, made another attempt at dating Stonehenge using astronomical calculations. Lockyer's method of computation was even more complex than Petrie's method had been. In fact, it was so complicated no one could duplicate it to see if it was accurate. Like Petrie's method, it was based on information that could only be assumed or guessed at. Still, Lockyer's estimates of a building date between 1880 and 1480 BCE were closer to most modern estimates.

Though neither Petrie's nor Lockyer's experiments were accurate, the publicity they received made the general public aware for the first time of Stonehenge's astronomical possibilities. They also showed scientists astronomy and mathematics might be a valid archaeological tool. More important at the time, Petrie's diagrams of Stonehenge were some of the most detailed that had ever been made. In making the diagrams, Petrie assigned a number to each stone. Stonehenge explorers and archaeologists have used this reference system ever since.

The sun rises behind Stonehenge during the summer solstice on June 21, 2010.

5

Protecting the Stones

Years of neglect and a rising flood of visitors had taken a toll on Stonehenge during the 1800s. By the late 1800s, some of the stones were leaning dangerously, and the area around the monument was battered and worn from overuse. Antiquarian and civic groups all over England began pushing for restoration of the site—or at least better management of it. Parliament discussed the possibility of taking Stonehenge as a national trust, which would make it a protected historic site.

By the turn of the twentieth century, tourists were wearing out the ancient stones, many of which were toppled or tilting.

> "Surely this thing unknowably old, of whose very form and purpose we have no sort of certainty, belongs to Time and Nature, and should be left to the pious operation of natural decay."[1]
>
> —FLINDERS PETRIE, IN A LETTER TO THE LONDON TIMES, 1901

The move was met with a storm of protest from wealthy landowners in the area. Upper-class English families had managed their own property for centuries, and the idea of government interference in their private affairs was unthinkable.

In the late 1800s, the Antrobus family owned the land Stonehenge stood on. The family blocked many attempts by the government to protect or improve the site. They also stopped all excavations in or near Stonehenge.

STONEHENGE FOR SALE

On December 31, 1900, a windstorm blew down one of Stonehenge's outer sarsen trilithons, breaking the lintel in half. These were the first stones to fall at the site since 1797. People flocked to Stonehenge from all over to see the damage and hunt for souvenirs. Shortly after, the Antrobus family enclosed Stonehenge in a fence and began charging an admission fee. By the end of 1901, more than 3,000 visitors had paid to visit Stonehenge under the supervision of local police. Still, nothing was done to upgrade the site or repair the damages to it.

MAINTENANCE AND MODERN DRUIDS

In the summer of 1901, local antiquarians noticed one of Stonehenge's sarsens was leaning and badly cracked. They feared it would soon break in half unless something was done. They begged the Antrobus family to let them stabilize the stone to prevent further damage. The family agreed and also granted the antiquarians permission to perform a small excavation during the restoration work.

Work began in September 1901. William Gowland, a local professor and former mining engineer, directed the stabilization of the leaning stones. He also performed a simple excavation that was the most precise and scientific done at Stonehenge up to that time. He kept detailed records of every inch of earth dug and every item found. All soil was sifted through fine mesh screens. Gowland found clear evidence the bluestones had been placed in their present positions after the sarsens were already in place. This was a question that no one had ever been able to answer before. In the dirt that had held stones upright, he found the tools of the builders, including hammerstones, deer antler picks, and flint axes—but no metallic objects.

DIGGING
DEEPER

Building Stonehenge

Gowland's excavation in 1901 shed new light on how Neolithic humans may have shaped and moved enormous stones. To break giant, rugged stone into manageable sizes, Gowland believed Stonehenge's builders would have used the fire and water method. This was a method used by ancient Mayans, Egyptians, Greeks, and Romans. The first step was to chip a groove in a stone where a clean break was needed. Then, a

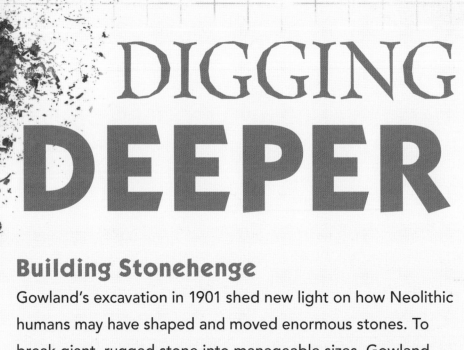

fire was built under the stone just below the groove. When the stone was intensely hot, cold water was poured over the groove, while workers with heavy stones or mallets pounded it. The combination of rapidly changing temperature and physical concussion would break the stone in a relatively straight line. Hammerstones of all sizes could then be used to chip, peck, and grind the surface of the stone into whatever shape the builders wanted.

Gowland's dig also showed how ancient people might have moved and lifted the stones. Evidence showed the builders had dug a hole with one side perfectly straight and the other side sloped sharply, like a ramp. The movers then pulled a stone on ropes over round logs to the hole and positioned its bottom over the ramp. Using timber levers, they moved the stone forward until gravity tilted its base down into the hole. Ropes and levers were then used to pull it upright. Stones and chalk earth were packed around the base.

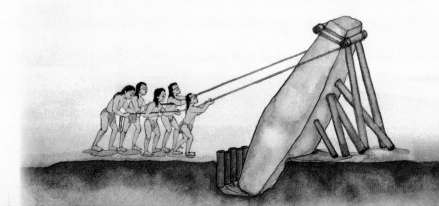

47

The builders, Gowland wrote, were clearly "the men of the Neolithic or . . . early Bronze Age."[2] He estimated a date of 1800 BCE for the building of the main stone structure.

At the beginning of the 1900s, people were becoming fascinated by Celtic culture. People began joining religious groups that claimed to be modern Druids. Two of these groups, the Ancient Order of Druids and the Church of the Universal Bond, designated Stonehenge as their official place of worship. They gathered there for meetings, particularly at the summer solstice. Little or nothing was known about ancient Druids or their rituals. There was no historical or archaeological evidence to suggest the original Druids had used Stonehenge. However, the members of the Druidic societies demanded their right to enter Stonehenge and use it when and how they saw fit.

WAR COMES TO STONEHENGE

World War I (1914–1918) changed everything. In 1913, Salisbury Plain, including the Antrobus estate, was turned over to the British military. Troop, aircraft, and artillery training facilities were built all around Stonehenge. The constant roar of big guns and tanks, the buzz of airplanes, and the pounding of thousands of boots daily threatened the ancient stones in ways no one in previous centuries could have imagined. On two occasions, the Bomb Squadron demanded the War Office tear down Stonehenge because it was

a hazard to low-flying aircraft. However, the stones were still standing by the end of the war in 1918. Left behind were hangars, vehicles, barracks, and weapon storage sheds.

The last Antrobus heir was killed in combat, so when Sir Edmund Antrobus died in 1915, no one was left to inherit the family estate. Once again, Stonehenge went up for sale. A Wiltshire man named Cecil Chubb bought the estate. In 1918, he gave the estate, Stonehenge included, to the British government.

6

More Discoveries

After World War I ended, the local Society of Antiquaries was appointed to evaluate Stonehenge and make recommendations about its restoration. British archaeologist Sir Arthur Evans headed a team of Great Britain's leading professional archaeologists. They proposed not only a restoration but also a thorough exploration of the entire site.

When World War I ended in 1918, Stonehenge was badly in need of repairs.

VOICES IN THE STONES

Researchers have found that Stonehenge's circular arrangement of stones would have had remarkable sound qualities. The size and placement of the stones when fully assembled would have created an echo effect similar to what is heard in large churches or concert halls. Voices would have seemed to come from many different directions. Scientists believe it is unlikely the stones were placed for this particular purpose. However, ancient people would certainly have noticed the effect.

In 1920, three dangerously leaning trilithons were taken down. The lintels were lifted off by a steam-powered crane, and the upright stones were hauled back into position. Three feet (0.9 m) of concrete was poured around their bases to ensure they would not sway again, and the lintels were lifted back into place.

MORE DIGGING

William Gowland, who led the admirable 1901 dig, had retired, so the society appointed his assistant, Colonel William Hawley, to head the excavation. An experienced excavator and Wiltshire native, Hawley was well liked, mainly because he had served as Stonehenge's chief guardian during the war. His efforts had frequently steered heavy military operations away from the teetering stones. Hawley was not given any instructions as to the exact purpose of his dig—only that he was to "excavate Stonehenge completely and at the minimum expense."[1]

Hawley began by looking into the holes of each upright stone when they were removed. He reported finding little of interest in any of the sarsen holes or in the wide surrounding ditch, which he also cleared. He lifted the Slaughter Stone and again found nothing, except a bottle of wine William Cunnington had buried there nearly 100 years earlier as a gift for future explorers.

R. S. Newall, Hawley's assistant, made a much more important discovery. Newall remembered seeing a drawing John Aubrey had made in 1666 that showed traces of a ring of cavities just inside the bank of Stonehenge's outer ditch. No one had noticed these before, so Newall decided to look for them at Stonehenge himself. He found a ring of 56 circular holes, which he called Aubrey Holes. They were 16 feet (4.9 m) apart all the way around the henge.[2] He excavated some of them and found that nearly all contained cremated remains and flint artifacts. However, none of the archaeologists involved in the dig could agree on exactly what the holes' original purpose might have been.

Hawley and Newall made no stunning discoveries, but they did add a few tantalizing bits of new information to the riddle of Stonehenge's building. Chips of bluestone, for instance, found in the filling around some of the sarsens, led them to conclude Stonehenge had not been built all at the same time. Probably, it had been erected in stages over many centuries. Hawley suggested three phases, though he had no real evidence for his suggestion. It turned out to be a good guess, as later investigations would prove.

Without any real direction or purpose, Hawley continued gathering scraps of bone, pottery, and flint for the next six years. The work grew tedious, and Hawley's reports, filed with the antiquarian society, showed his discouragement. In one of them, he commented that the meaning of what he found was a "puzzle like everything else here."[3] Hawley told a reporter, "The more we dig, the more the mystery appears to deepen." His final report concluded, "It is to be hoped that future excavators will be able to throw more light upon [Stonehenge] than I have done."[4]

Hawley's excavation damaged the Stonehenge site. A large area of the ground was once again disturbed, and items were scattered without purpose. Some of the relics and artifacts found went to museums, but much of what was found during the 1919–1926 digs was later reburied in holes in and around Stonehenge.

THE STORY OF THE STONES

While Hawley was still at work, geologist H. H. Thomas made an important discovery. He was able to pinpoint the exact source of the rocks used at Stonehenge. It was widely accepted that the sarsen sandstones had come from Marlborough, Wiltshire, approximately 20 miles (32 km) north of the site. However, people still did not know where ancient masons had gotten the bluestones. In 1923, Thomas studied bluestone samples collected at Stonehenge by Cunnington and others. He then searched for the most likely places these stones might have originated. The closest match he found was samples of stones other geologists had gathered in the Preseli Mountains of Wales, 150 miles (240 km) from Salisbury Plain. Thomas even believed he had pinpointed the specific quarry the bluestones must have come from. He also concluded that the Altar Stone, a different variety of sandstone from the sarsens, came from another site in those same mountains. Although Thomas's exact location has since been called into question, his proof that Stonehenge's

Many of Stonehenge's bluestones may have come from a quarry at Carn Meini, Wales, in the Preseli Mountains.

DID GLACIERS MOVE THE STONES?

The discovery that the bluestones had been moved from Wales raised many questions. It seemed impossible that ancient humans would have had the technology to transport four-short-ton (3.6 metric ton) bluestones hundreds of miles.[5] Archaeologist Aubrey Burl has suggested Ice Age glaciers may have been responsible for moving the massive stones from Wales to the area near Stonehenge. However, most scientists do not support his theory.

builders brought bluestones from Wales is still accepted today.

Thomas also saw what he thought was evidence many of the bluestones at Stonehenge had been hand-shaped more than once. Thomas theorized the Stonehenge bluestones could have been the components of another ancient circle in Wales. This site might once have held great meaning for people of that area and beyond. Perhaps at some point, the people of that region moved east to Salisbury, where they decided to build a similar monument. To invest it with greater meaning, they may have decided to retrieve old stones from their former home and bring them to the new site.

DISCOVERIES FROM THE AIR

Also in 1923, while archaeologist O. G. S. Crawford was looking through old negatives of photos taken during the war, he made a startling discovery. The Air Corps had frequently photographed Stonehenge and the surrounding area while training aerial photographers. As a result, there were hundreds of aerial photos of the site and surrounding area. One of these photos clearly showed two parallel lines running cross-country from Stonehenge toward the east. These lines, the man realized, were the Avenue ditches William Stukeley had first described in 1721. At that time, Stukeley had been able to trace the Avenue a short distance before he lost it in newly plowed fields. The photograph showed the Avenue running to the east and taking a sharp turn south, where it ended at the River Avon, approximately 2.5 miles (4 km) from Stonehenge.[6]

Two years later, a pilot flying over Salisbury Plain noticed an unusual circular indentation in the earth not far from Stonehenge. He was high enough to see Stonehenge and the new circle.

A 1925 photo shows Stonehenge from the air.

DIGGING
DEEPER

A Stone-Moving Experience

Several experiments have been done over the years to see if moving heavy stones across land and water might be possible. One of these took place in 1954, when archaeologist Richard Atkinson recruited a group of English schoolboys to row a boat laden with a small bluestone on the River Avon. Although the schoolboys were able to move the stones, the event, which broadcast on television, did not prove much. Still, many viewers found it immensely entertaining.

The Welsh group Menter Preseli took on a much more serious and ambitious project in 2000. This group set out to move a more than three-short-ton (2.7 metric ton)

Some archaeologists believe Stonehenge's builders moved the great stones by rolling them on enormous logs.

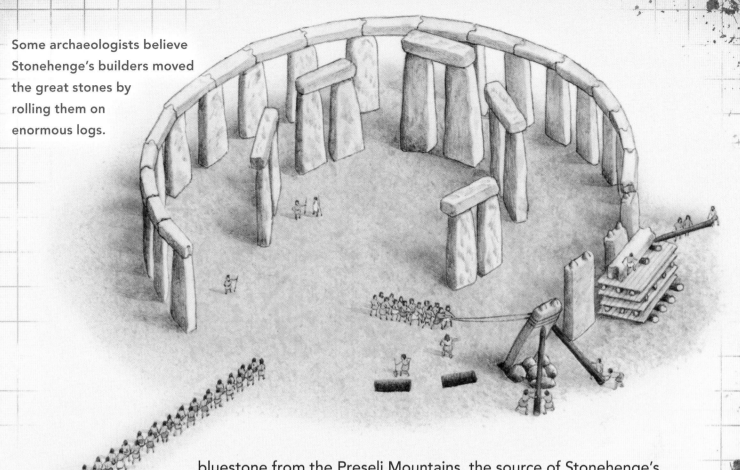

bluestone from the Preseli Mountains, the source of Stonehenge's bluestones, to Salisbury, using only Stone Age methods.[7] The team had trouble levering and rolling the stone from the start. At one point, it even slipped off rafts and sank in Bristol Channel between Wales and England. When the project was finally abandoned two years later, the stone had been moved more times by modern means, including cranes, tugboats, modern rope, and nets, than by prehistoric means. The conclusion was that Stone Age people simply knew much more about moving stones that modern people do.

He could see they were nearly the same size and shape. Ground examination revealed a henge approximately the same size as Stonehenge. Like Stonehenge, it had an entrance opening on the northeastern side. Inside the ditch were several sets of holes forming inner circles, quite similar to Stonehenge. However, there were no standing stones at this new circle. From imprints left in the holes by ancient tree bark, investigators knew the holes had once held timber posts, arranged in a pattern that suggested a wooden shelter. The physical similarities between Stonehenge and this new circle were so clear, the site was named Woodhenge.

After this, flyers began seeing henge circles all around the area. Not far from Woodhenge, someone spotted a huge circle nearly 1,640 feet (500 m) in diameter.[8] It was named Durrington Walls. Nothing appeared to have been built inside it, so there was no real investigation of the site. However, these new henges proved Stonehenge was not alone in the region's landscape.

SAVING STONEHENGE

By the late 1920s, Stonehenge was once again in danger. Various surrounding landowners had begun development near the site. A highway had actually been paved through one part of Stonehenge's ditch. Many of the army's World War I buildings were still nearby, rusting and rotting to pieces.

Several businesses had opened near the henge, including a pig farm and a restaurant. Preservationists and antiquarians grew more and more alarmed.

In 1927, landowners on all sides of Stonehenge agreed to sell their land if someone came up with the money. The Stonehenge Protection Committee was organized, and it set in motion an enthusiastic national campaign to raise the funds. Newspaper and radio appeals urged British citizens to give money to help save Stonehenge before it was too late. Even King George V contributed

LEY LINES AND UFOS

Since the earliest days, people have suspected something supernatural was going on in and around Stonehenge. The region is known for an unusual number of UFO sightings. One of the most famous supernatural supporters was businessman and antiquarian Alfred Watkins. In 1921, he claimed to have discovered an invisible network of perfectly straight lines he called leys. He believed ancient surveyors had laid them out as trade routes. Watkins felt certain leys connected important ancient sites, creating a kind of invisible road map ancients could follow. In the mid-1900s, the idea of leys took on a more supernatural meaning. Some people claimed Stonehenge and other ancient sites lie at intersections of ley lines. At these points, the earth's power is concentrated and flows outward along the leys like electricity through wires. Some people think frequent UFO sightings reported near Stonehenge are proof that alien beings recognize and use leys or some other power source in the area.

and joined in the push that eventually raised enough money to secure the land around the site.

In 1929, 1,500 acres (607 ha) of additional land around Stonehenge was purchased and presented to the National Trust.[9] Workers and volunteers from all over Great Britain hurried to the Salisbury Plain to help tear down old military buildings and restore the land to its original condition.

Two buildings closest to Stonehenge were left in place, temporarily. These housed the huge assortment of items discovered and stored in cloth bags by Hawley during his 1919–1926 excavations. Before he left, he had hurriedly reburied some artifacts. However, other finds remained, and nobody seemed to know what to do with them.

Eventually, some of the finds were divided among various museums, including Oxford and the British Museum. The rest were unceremoniously reburied in and around Stonehenge. The final bag was emptied into Aubrey Hole No. 7, with a plaque stating why the material was there. It was an anticlimactic end to the largest excavation in the history of Stonehenge.

Despite the best efforts by the National Trust to return the land around Stonehenge to its premodern condition, problems worsened in the 1930s. The busy public road still passed within a few yards of the stones.

Preservationists wanted it removed, but the government could not afford to build another road somewhere else.

The popular fund-raising campaign of the late 1920s had drawn a great deal of attention to Stonehenge. In the 1930s, the site became a wildly popular tourist destination. Approximately 15,000 people routinely visited during each summer month, and summer solstice celebrations drew huge crowds.[10] Parked cars belonging to the site's tourists often blocked highways. In 1935, the British government installed a parking lot across the road, but nobody used it. It was easier and closer to park at the roadside.

Traffic near Stonehenge brought constant noise, vibration, and pollution that threatened the old stones.

Stonehenge Decoded?

Around 1950, a trio of archaeologists—Richard Atkinson, Stuart Piggott and J. F. S. Stone—joined to reexamine the notes and papers of Hawley's excavation. They then published a long-overdue report on the dig, along with a list of finds. By the 1950s, the location of most of the artifacts was unknown, since they had been reburied in unmarked holes all around Stonehenge.

A photographer captures elevated shots of some of Stonehenge's holes during a 1954 excavation.

DATES AND DAGGERS

The team dug deep into Aubrey Hole No. 32, which had never been examined, and retrieved a piece of charcoal. They sent this sample to the lab of Willard Libby at the University of Chicago to be analyzed. In the 1940s, Libby had invented a new method for determining the dates of material from ancient sites. The process, called radiocarbon dating, was revolutionizing archaeological research. For the first time in history, archaeologists had a reliable method of determining how old ancient relics really were. The results of Libby's test showed the piece of charcoal

RADIOCARBON DATING

Willard Libby discovered that during photosynthesis, plants absorb an element called radioactive carbon, or carbon-14. When animals eat the plants, they absorb the carbon-14 from the plants. After a plant or animal dies, its store of carbon-14 begins to decay at a regular rate. This decay can be measured using the half-life of carbon. An element's half-life is the time it takes for one-half of that element to decay. The half-life of carbon is 5,730 years. By figuring out how much carbon-14 was left in a sample of a once-living object, Libby could discover how old that sample was. Radiocarbon dating can be used on any organic material, including bone, cloth, wood, and more. The process gave archaeologists and other scientists an incredible new tool that allowed them to see into the past as never before.

dated from approximately 1850 BCE. This matched most experts' views that Stonehenge was Neolithic, built between 2000 and 1500 BCE.

In 1953, while doing a photographic survey of the sarsen stones, Atkinson made a startling discovery. Through his camera's viewfinder, he noticed the carving of a knife or dagger on one of the stones. It looked a great deal like metal daggers made and used during the Bronze Age. Closer examination revealed other carvings. Some of these were in the shape of axes, the kind used in Ireland in ancient times. Like most discoveries at Stonehenge, however, what these carvings meant was a matter of opinion.

A SEQUENCE OF EVENTS

After the invention of radiocarbon dating, no one was ever able to look at Stonehenge in the same way. In 1956, Atkinson published a book titled *Stonehenge*, which drew together previously known information about the ancient site and new discoveries just beginning to be understood. In his book, Atkinson presented the theory that Stonehenge as a monument had been built in three stages. Based on the stone carvings he found in 1953, he had already decided Stonehenge must have been built during the Bronze Age, from approximately 2000 to 1000 BCE. Atkinson based many of his dates on radiocarbon dating, which was still new and somewhat experimental. He received various dates from different radiocarbon dating tests, but he chose to accept only the dates that supported his original theory.

Atkinson believed the ancient people who built Stonehenge had been farmers and herders, whose ancestors probably cleared Salisbury Plain of trees to make fields for crops. The ancestors may have built the Cursus and several nearby henge circles. Many of the long barrows, the earliest burials found around the area, were also theirs. After many of these features were in place in the late Neolithic period, people began building the earliest phase of Stonehenge.

According to Atkinson, the first stage of Stonehenge circle, Stonehenge 1, was basically an earthwork circle with a ditch and bank around it, and

THE GENIUS OF MYCENAE

The dagger Atkinson found carved on the stones was not like any known to be in England in the Neolithic era. But it was very similar to a style common in ancient Greece, particularly at royal tombs in Mycenae, a major center of Greek civilization. This led Atkinson to believe Stonehenge must have been the work of some ancient genius of Mycenae who had migrated from the Mediterranean region to England. Atkinson and others believed the dagger images in the stones were a kind of signature placed there by the ancient architect to show his true heritage. However, Atkinson's Mycenae idea was never widely accepted.

it was a causeway entrance. He set the date of this construction as happening between 1900 and 1700 BCE. The next phase of building, Stonehenge 2, which Atkinson believed took place roughly between 1700 to 1600 BCE, was a remodeling of the first phase. Like Stonehenge 1, traces of 2 can be found only in excavated evidence. Nothing of its structure remains in plain view today. During this stage of development, the site's axis was shifted a little more to the east, and construction on the Avenue began. Later, possibly hundreds of years after Stonehenge 2 was completed, the stone structure that is recognized today was built in several stages between 1500 and 1400 BCE.

About a century or so later, Atkinson asserted, the bluestones that had been removed from Stonehenge 2 were returned and set up inside the sarsen horseshoe. He believed this horseshoe included at least two bluestone trilithons. Not long after the horseshoe was assembled, the bluestones were taken down and rearranged into the two groups we see today. Atkinson noted that during the later years of Stage 3,

FINAL RESTORATIONS

In 1958, the British government began a long-awaited overhaul of Stonehenge. Using a huge crane, workers reset stones that had fallen in 1797 and 1900 back into their original positions. In 1959, three badly leaning upright stones were also restored. While doing so, however, another stone was bumped and weakened. It toppled four years later and was quickly restored. This returned Stonehenge to descriptions of its appearance in the 1500s, and nothing more has been done since.

the focus of the builders seemed to waver. They dug a number of holes outside the sarsen circle and then filled them in. And at one point, they appeared to have pulled down previously arranged bluestones and completely rearranged them. It is unlikely anyone will ever know why.

One final change that occurred during this period was the extension of the Avenue another 1.5 miles (2.4 km) to the River Avon at West Amesbury.[1] The reason for this suggested to Atkinson yet another shift in cultural or religious practice.

To figure all this out, particularly the order in which stones were erected and moved, Atkinson used a variety of clues and a great deal of logic. The most obvious clues were clear marks, holes, and indentations left behind when stones were dug out and moved. Chips of stone from one kind of rock in the bottom of a hole containing another sometimes showed a change had

POSTS IN A PARKING LOT PROVIDE A NEW DATE

In 1966, archaeologists made an exciting discovery. Before a new parking lot was installed near Stonehenge, archaeologists excavated ground that had never been investigated. Deep below the surface, they found postholes in which timber posts had once stood. Scientists were stunned when charcoal in one of the holes dated one of the posts to between 8820 and 7730 BCE. Nothing this old had been found at the site before. In 1988, tests were conducted on another hole found at the same site. These tests indicated the posts were built between 7480 and 6950 BCE. The postholes suggested people built something close to the site 4,000 to 5,000 years before any construction of Stonehenge started.

been made. The size of holes in which stones stood was another clue. Some holes were too large for their present stone and contained a lot of dirt and debris to fill in the extra space. Other holes showed clear signs they had been widened to fit larger stones. By carbon dating organic material he found among the new and old fill, Atkinson was able to determine approximate dates that allowed him to guess what might have been moved when. However, by the 1980s, newer and better carbon dating methods had moved Atkinson's 1950s dates back by thousands of years.

THE BIRTH OF ARCHAEOASTRONOMY

William Stukeley's observation that one could stand at the center of Stonehenge, facing east, and watch the midsummer sun rise above the horizon just over the Heel Stone had fascinated people for years. By the 1960s, scientists generally believed ancient people may have annually gathered at Stonehenge for that purpose, perhaps even for religious rituals relating to the sun or the turning of the seasons. Lockyer's and Petrie's experiments in the late 1800s had been based on this idea, even if their mathematics were questionable. Astronomer Gerald Hawkins took this idea to a whole new level. When it appeared in 1965, Hawkins's book, *Stonehenge Decoded*, claimed the circle was not just an astronomical observatory but also an ancient computer, capable of many different astronomical calculations.

Stonehenge's position on an open plain provided a mostly unobstructed view of the whole sky. Hawkins envisioned ancient astronomers standing inside the stone circle, staring up and out along or between various stones, lining them up with rising or setting planets, stars, the sun and moon, and other celestial objects. Using natural features, such as outlying rocks or small hills in the distance, the way a shooter uses a gun sight, ancient people could keep careful track of all sorts of sky events. Hawkins claimed to have discovered 165 solar, lunar, and stellar alignments ancient people could have made, using Stonehenge and surrounding features as an astronomical instrument.

Hawkins was a well-known scientist and the head of the astronomy department at the University of Boston. His claims caused quite a sensation. The implications were stunning. If true, Hawkins's assertion suggested the Stone Age builders of Stonehenge "knew more about the motions of the sun and moon in the heavens than most scholars do today."[2]

Stonehenge Decoded sold millions of copies and made Hawkins a celebrity. However, scientists, particularly archaeologists, were skeptical. Dozens of archaeologists accused Hawkins of faulty reasoning. Atkinson could not accept the fact that many of Hawkins's supposed Stonehenge sight points were

DURRINGTON WALLS

In 1967, work was scheduled to begin on widening the highway northeast of Stonehenge. The new construction would cut straight through Durrington Walls. The massive henge had been discovered in the 1920s, but it was never explored. Before roadwork began, archaeologist Geoffrey Wainwright bulldozed the site himself. Beneath tons of soil, he found evidence of two smaller circles. Everywhere he looked, he found piles of animal bones and pottery. Road crews soon arrived to pave the roadway over his trenches. It would not be until the early 2000s that more information about Durrington Walls came to light.

natural features—shapeless depressions in the earth, distant hilltops, and others. Atkinson concluded that if these were removed, few of Hawkins' alignments made any sense. On the other side, astronomers mostly supported Hawkins. They claimed archaeologists simply did not understand the difficult mathematics behind astronomical alignments. Some astronomers hinted archaeologists were jealous someone from a different branch of science had solved Stonehenge's toughest riddle.

The controversy raged for years. During that time, nearly every ancient site in the world was studied, from Central America to Egypt, and some amazing new discoveries were made. By the 1990s, enough evidence had been collected that most archaeologists came to accept Hawkins's basic ideas. Not all of his alignments held up to closer examination, but research had revealed that ancient people had been capable of advanced thinking. Ancient cultures actually had used natural features as sight lines to track astronomical events. Hawkins's book is now recognized as groundbreaking. It introduced a whole new field of scientific investigation called archaeoastronomy.

Many archaeologists believe Stonehenge was intended to be an ancient observatory that predicted astronomical events.

8

Stonehenge for All

In 1974, a wild and noisy party, the Stonehenge Free Festival, was held only a few hundred yards from the stones. Ending on June 21, the summer solstice, the festival featured music and other activities. The event drew thousands of people from all over the world. Aside from mountains of trash and monumental traffic problems, the event was mostly peaceful. It became an annual event. However when more than 100,000 people attended in 1984, authorities declared the festival would not

Stonehenge has become a popular site for modern Druids.

THE STONEHENGE ARCHER

In 1978, archaeologists Richard Atkinson and J. G. Evans made a remarkable discovery. While digging in a section of Stonehenge's outer ditch, they found the burial site of a man killed in approximately 2300 BCE. Flint arrowheads were still embedded in his bones, indicating the man had been riddled with arrows. He was wearing a stone wrist guard similar to the kind archers once wore, earning him the nickname "the Stonehenge Archer." For years, people have pondered the meaning of the man's death and the placement of his body. Was he killed valiantly in battle and honored by being buried at a sacred place? Or was he an outcast or criminal, executed for some crime and thrown into the ditch as a sacrificial gift to gods or spirits? Scientists still have not solved the mystery of the Stonehenge Archer.

be held again. They argued the event was becoming unsafe—both for the stones and the attendees. Stonehenge would now be closed to the public on the summer solstice.

In June 1985, riot police met would-be festivalgoers at the Wiltshire border. The resulting Battle of the Beanfield, as the confrontation came to be called, was an ugly, much-publicized incident that resulted in injuries on both sides and dozens of arrests. Protestors claimed police brutality and violation of their rights. Police charged protesters with trespassing, disorderly conduct, and resisting arrest. While courts later ruled the police were guilty of using excessive force, exactly what happened that day is still largely a matter of opinion.

PRESERVING STONEHENGE

Each year, the United Nations Educational, Scientific and Cultural Organization (UNESCO) selects important and irreplaceable cultural sites around the world it believes deserve protection and preservation. In 1986, Stonehenge was designated as a UNESCO World Heritage Site. The organization English Heritage would oversee Stonehenge's upkeep and safety. Also, as a result of Stonehenge's new status, Parliament passed the Public Order Act. This new act gave police full authority to keep people away from public monuments, particularly Stonehenge.

However, none of these measures stopped protesters who wanted to celebrate the summer solstice at Stonehenge. Thousands of modern-day Druids joined these protesters, claiming their religious right to worship at Stonehenge was being illegally violated. For the 1989 summer solstice, English Heritage set up a four-mile (6.4 km) circle of security, including riot police, helicopters, and razor wire fencing, around Stonehenge. Similar yearly standoffs and arrests continued until 1995.

In the mid-1990s, police and security guards began working with Stonehenge visitors to protect the stones.

In 1996, new leadership at English Heritage decided to try a softer approach. They removed most fencing from around Stonehenge, and walkways were installed around—but not inside—the stone circle. Signs requested visitors stay on the pathways and respect the delicate nature of the site. Security officers were always present to keep people from touching or climbing on the stones, but they used a more welcoming, far less aggressive approach with visitors, acting more as guides than guards. In 2000, Stonehenge was reopened to the public during the summer solstice. Crowds still flock each year to Stonehenge to witness the rising sun at summer solstice, but they are usually peaceful and respectful of the ancient stones.

NEW WAYS TO EXPLORE

The dawning of the 2000s saw more than a physical renewal for Stonehenge. Archaeological exploration entered a new era, as well. In 1995, English Heritage supervised the publication of the largest archive of past knowledge about Stonehenge that had ever been gathered. The impact of this monumental work, called *Stonehenge in Its Landscape*, was enormous. For the first time scientists and researchers of all kinds could get information and data that had never been available to them before.

At the same time, archaeologists were gaining other new tools that were drastically changing the way they worked. No longer was excavation the only way to find out what was underground or lying hidden on the surface. Archaeologists now had far better ways of seeing and measuring archaeological sites. Satellite imaging takes photos from space. This gives archaeologists a chance to observe minor changes in a landscape that might indicate a buried structure. They may have never spotted these changes up close. Geographic Information Systems (GIS) allows archaeologists to map and analyze archaeological sites. GIS uses Global Positioning Systems (GPS) to get exact coordinates for sites. Infrared photography allows archaeologists to take aerial photos that show objects or structures buried underground. Laser scanning allows archaeologists to quickly measure the exact distance to an object. By taking many measurements of archaeological sites, archaeologists can even create 3-D models of structures that may have stood there.

The development of lightweight portable technology also allowed archaeologists to find and study artifacts like never before. Magnetometry helps archaeologists find buried artifacts by measuring the magnetism patterns in soil. Ground-penetrating radar also helps archaeologists locate structures and objects under the

DEER ANTLERS

One of the most common finds at Stonehenge and other henges is an abundance of deer antlers. These were used as picks by the teams of builders digging the deep ditches and holes. Such work would have been difficult and would have taken a long time. Fortunately, for modern scientists, many of these tools broke during construction. Workers tossed the antlers into dirt piles, ditches, or holes made by workers. Because the antlers contain traces of carbon-14, scientists can radiocarbon date the antlers. This provides them with clues about the approximate date when a specific part of the site was built.

soil. Radiocarbon dating, DNA testing, and chemical analysis tools provide new ways to examine plant and human remains. Computers can be used to analyze this data. Just as important as new technology were new ways of thinking. The real value of *Stonehenge in Its Landscape* was that it encouraged scientists to think about Stonehenge not just as a single, isolated structure but rather as part of a group of sites that were closely interconnected.

STATION STONES

The Station Stones are four stones that appear to form the four corners of a perfect rectangle. The rectangle extends from the northwest side to the southeast side of the Aubrey Hole circle. Only two of the four stones still exist, and one of the survivors is badly worn. The rectangular layout of the Station Stones is unusual, since everything else about Stonehenge seems to be laid out with a circular design in mind. Nobody knows for certain what they were, but they have been shown to have astronomical alignments with the rising and setting moon.

9

The Riverside Project

In the 2000s, archaeologist Mike Parker Pearson began a new excavation project that would make great strides in solving the mystery of Stonehenge's purpose. He believed clues to this mystery could be uncovered at Durrington Walls. In 1991, Parker Pearson had been working on a research project in Madagascar. He worked with and befriended Ramilisonina, a native archaeologist of that island. In 1998, Ramilisonina came to visit Parker Pearson, who

In the 2000s, new investigations of Stonehenge and nearby Durrington Walls brought startling discoveries.

was by then a professor at the University of Sheffield. During Ramilisonina's visit, Parker Pearson took his friend to see Stonehenge.

A NEW THEORY

Ramilisonina was surprised when Parker Pearson mentioned he had no idea what the stones had been used for. In Madagascar, Ramilisonina explained, stone monuments are always built to honor dead ancestors. Wood, plant, and animal products are materials for the use of the living during their time on Earth, because they decompose after death. Stone, hard and unyielding to time and rot, is meant for the dead. Ramilisonina believed Stonehenge had been built as a place to remember and honor the dead.

Parker Pearson began considering his friend's comments. Burial mounds and barrows were everywhere around the site. The buried ashes of many ancient cremations had been found inside the henge. This all suggested that Stonehenge was the middle of a huge ancient cemetery. The area was also home to other ancient henges, such as Durrington Walls, which were known to have once contained huge wooden structures. Parker Pearson thought it was possible that, in ancient times, wood and stone had the same meaning Ramilisonina said they still held in his country. If so, the wooden henges were places for the living, and the stone henges were places for the dead.

MIKE PARKER PEARSON

As a boy, Mike Parker Pearson loved searching for fossils among the driveway pebbles of his family's home in southwest England. When he was six, he found the book *Fun With Archaeology* in his local library, and the book changed his life. When he visited Stonehenge with his parents, he thought everything that could be known about the stones must have already been discovered. Little did he know that he would come back one day as an archaeologist and unlock many of its toughest secrets. Parker Pearson and his team focused on excavating an ancient village at Durrington Walls, which he believed was directly connected to Stonehenge.

A Neolithic village at Durrington Walls

Parker Pearson felt evidence supporting this new theory might be waiting at Durrington Walls. In 2003, he organized the Stonehenge Riverside Project to study the area around Stonehenge, generally west of the River Avon. The project eventually involved more than 30 of the world's leading experts in archaeology and ancient studies. It was one of the largest teams ever assembled to investigate the Stonehenge landscape.

Parker Pearson was searching for evidence that ancient people had built Stonehenge and Durrington Walls to represent two stages of existence—life and death. With its burials and massive stone architecture, Stonehenge's connection to death was clear. To support Parker Pearson's theory, the Stonehenge Riverside Project needed to find evidence the wooden structures and activities at Durrington Walls symbolized the world of the living. Most important, they needed to prove the same people had used the two sites at the same time.

Parker Pearson already knew some things about Durrington Walls. That circle, only three miles (1.9 km) from Stonehenge, had long fascinated him.[1] In 1967, Geoffrey Wainwright had discovered many wooden posts that had once made up part of the site known as Durrington's Southern Circle. It was clearly a place where large numbers of people had gathered and perhaps lived. Parker Pearson needed a connection between Durrington Walls and Stonehenge, and he believed that connection was the River Avon.

The Avenue connected Stonehenge to this important river. Parker Pearson thought there might be a similar pathway connecting Durrington Walls to the River Avon.

LAND OF THE LIVING, LAND OF THE DEAD

Parker Pearson and his team began work at Durrington Walls in 2003. Digging promptly revealed pits full of animal bones, the remains of ancient feasts. These finds were interesting, but they did not prove much on their own. Then in 2005, Parker Pearson and his team began finding evidence of dozens of houses. These had floors made of hard-packed chalk plaster, fire pits, and postholes. They

Rivers, such as the Avon, held great symbolism for ancient humans.

would have been small but comfortable dwellings, part of a large village covering 42 acres (17 ha).[2] At one time, thousands of people might have lived in the village.

Litter left from the feasting also contained an important clue. The garbage piles contained a large number of pig bones. When these were analyzed, nearly all were shown to be from pigs no more than nine months old. Since pigs are usually born in the spring, this suggested to the team the pigs were killed and eaten in winter. This meant the feasts took place in midwinter, suggesting the winter solstice held as much importance for ancient people as the summer solstice.

During excavation in 2005, the team discovered something. Most of the postholes were enormous, as much as three feet (0.9 m) wide, suggesting the timbers they had held had also been huge.[3] To cut down such massive trees with Stone Age axes would have been incredibly hard. To drag them to the site and lift them upright would have been even harder. Additionally, the general size and layout of the Durrington Southern Circle was almost identical to that of Stonehenge. The only difference was that stones had been installed in Stonehenge's holes and massive timber posts clearly had stood in the Southern Circle. Some holes still showed the outline of the trees' bark, markings archaeologists call post-pipes. Also the axis of the Southern Circle was southwest, not northeast, as it was at Stonehenge. This wooden structure had faced the winter sunset—the mirror image of Stonehenge's summer sunrise alignment.

The pieces of the puzzle were beginning to come together for Parker Pearson. From 2005 to 2006, the Riverside team unearthed a hard-packed pathway, carefully paved with broken pieces of stone, animal bones, and pottery fragments. It was 100 feet (30.5 m) wide and ended at the Avon.[4] Here at last was

WRITTEN IN BONE

Archeologists can learn where a person was born by looking at his or her bones. Nearly all rocks have a little bit of the element strontium. However, the isotope, or variation, of strontium is different in different types of rocks. Humans ingest strontium through water and plants, and traces of the element end up in their bones. By studying the strontium in human bones, archaeologists can determine the geologic region in which a person lived. Since different human bones develop at different times, archaeologists can even tell how a person may have moved around during his or her life. For example, since teeth form when a person is young, archaeologists can study the ratio of strontium isotopes in teeth to learn where a person spent his or her childhood. Graves in the Stonehenge area contain the remains of many people who apparently suffered serious illnesses or injuries while alive. Tests on bones revealed some were born as far away as mainland Europe. Some archaeologists believe this suggests ancient people journeyed to Stonehenge, hoping to be cured.

91

Archaeologists have been able to excavate the clay floors of Neolithic houses at Durrington Walls.

the connection Parker Pearson had been looking for.

In 2009, the Riverside team found yet another henge at the very end of Stonehenge's Avenue on the Avon. This circle was found to have once contained 25 standing bluestones, which had long since vanished. The team named the site Bluestonehenge. Radiocarbon dating showed it was from the 2900s BCE. Parker Pearson had found a similar age when he used radiocarbon dating to determine the age of the Durrington Walls' Southern Circle.

Parker Pearson and his team agreed the connection between these sites was clear. Ancient people had used them as part of special midwinter ceremonies held each year. Stonehenge, with its stones surrounding burials, represented the domain of the dead. Durrington, with its wooden structures and emphasis on feasting, represented the realm of the living.

The team envisioned people moving in solemn seasonal marches from one ritual site to the other. Each site was aligned differently to the sun. Parker Pearson theorized ancient people would have watched the midsummer sunrise at Stonehenge and then walked solemnly along the river and up the Avenue to Durrington's Southern Circle, where they would observe summer sunset. At midwinter, they would reverse course. The purpose of these ritual processions was likely to honor dead ancestors, as Ramilisonina had suggested. Perhaps the ashes of special leaders were carried from Durrington to Stonehenge during these ceremonies. Parker Pearson suggested the remains of lesser important people were cast into the river, which was also sacred.

PERFECT TIMING

Using the latest technology, particularly better radiocarbon dating, the Riverside Project team was finally able to accomplish what no other investigation in the past had been able to do. They were able to identify specific dates for the various phases Stonehenge had gone through over the centuries. Along the way, they recognized key mistakes other investigators before them had made. This was mostly because those earlier explorers did not find or misunderstood important evidence. In addition, they simply did not have the advanced tools the 2000s team had. The new sequence of events the Riverside Project found was much older than anyone previously could have imagined.

The earliest phase of Stonehenge, Stage 1, was built between 3000 and 2920 BCE. This was mainly a simple ditch and bank enclosure with the Aubrey Holes containing 56 standing bluestones. An arrangement of timber posts and standing stones was also erected inside and outside the enclosure. This arrangement, the Riverside team found, allowed someone standing at the center of the circle to pinpoint the place on the horizon where the midsummer sun rose each year. From another central viewpoint, observers were also able to mark the location of an important moonrise.

Stage 2 took place between 2620 and 2480 BCE. During this phase, builders erected five trilithons, a double arc of bluestones, the sarsen circle, and a large gatelike structure of sarsen stones at the entrance. One of these stones fell at some point and became the Slaughter Stone.

During Stage 3, between 2480 and 2280 BCE, the Avenue was laid out along ridges that were already aligned toward the rising midsummer sun. Parker Pearson and his team strongly suspected it was this natural landscape feature that probably led ancient people to build a monument here in the first place.

Stage 4, between 2280 and 2020 BCE, was mainly a remodeling of Stage 3, with bluestones rearranged into the outer bluestone circle and a center oval. Others, including Atkinson, had thought ancient people intentionally moved some of these central bluestones to create the inner horseshoe, most of which is still in place today. Parker Pearson's excavations revealed the stones had been taken away in historical times, during the Roman period, most likely. This was just one example they found of widespread removal and damage at Stonehenge done in Roman and medieval times.

"Techniques improve all the time, and every generation of archaeologists curses the work of those before them. If only they had left well alone, or had had access to the sophisticated analytical methods of today. Half of Stonehenge was dug up during the twentieth century alone; one day, there may be nothing left undisturbed for the archaeologists of the future."[5]

—MIKE PARKER PEARSON, 2012

During Stage 5, from 1680 to 1520 BCE, the only additions to Stonehenge were two rings of rectangular holes, known as Y and Z holes, dug just outside the sarsen circle. These large, mysterious holes remained open and empty, except for items such as deer antlers, some of which were centuries old when placed there. Over the centuries, the holes filled up with silt, much of it blown in from surrounding fields. To Parker Pearson and his colleagues, the Y and Z holes held great significance. This period, from 1680 to 1520 BCE, was the middle of the Bronze Age in England, a time when people began laying out field boundaries. It was also an age when tomb and monument building suddenly stopped. The Riverside team recognized these ancient, empty holes suggested there was a moment when community goals of working to honor dead ancestors changed to individual goals, where people began focusing on working for the benefit of their own living relatives. Gradually, according to Parker Pearson, Stonehenge became "a relic of a bygone age" and began its decline into the ruin we know today.[6]

AN ENDURING PUZZLE

The Stonehenge Riverside Project officially lasted from 2003 to 2009. During those years, thousands of physical objects were collected, including artifacts and relics and soil, rock, and bone samples. The team also gathered a stunning amount of technical data, measurements, and other information. All of this data will take years of careful study to fully understand. New discoveries likely lie in computer databases, labs, and collection boxes, waiting to be recognized.

Some scientists have suggested Stonehenge is a puzzle without a solution, which may be the real reason the site continues to fascinate people thousands of years after it was made.

After centuries of study, much about Stonehenge still remains mysterious.

TIMELINE

8820–7730 BCE

Hunter-gatherer people on Salisbury Plain erect timber posts near the site of Stonehenge.

3000–1520 BCE

Stonehenge is built in five stages.

1136 CE

Geoffrey of Monmouth writes *The History of the Kings of Britain*, which suggests Merlin the Magician is responsible for building Stonehenge.

1660s

John Aubrey investigates Stonehenge and begins writing *Monumenta Britannica*.

1721–1724

William Stukeley surveys Stonehenge and the surrounding area.

1919–1926

Colonel William Hawley excavates at Stonehenge; his assistant discovers the Aubrey Holes.

1940s

Willard Libby develops the radiocarbon dating process.

1965

Gerald Hawkins's *Stonehenge Decoded* claims Stonehenge was an ancient astronomical instrument.

1966

Ancient timber postholes are found under the Stonehenge parking lot.

1986

The United Nations Educational, Scientific and Cultural Organization (UNESCO) designates Stonehenge as a World Heritage Site.

1995

English Heritage publishes *Stonehenge in Its Landscape*, an archive of previous research and knowledge of Stonehenge.

2003–2009

Mike Parker Pearson leads the Stonehenge Riverside Project, pinpointing dates for the site's construction.

DIGGING UP THE FACTS

DATE OF DISCOVERY

Locals have always known about Stonehenge. One of the earliest excavations was organized by the Duke of Buckingham in 1620.

KEY PLAYERS

- John Aubrey was the first to seriously explore Stonehenge and compare it to other stone circles in England.

- Richard Atkinson was the archaeologist who advanced the understanding of Stonehenge and made guesses about its age.

- Mike Parker Pearson was the archaeologist and leader of the Riverside Project team that established Stonehenge's true age and sequence of construction as is generally accepted today.

KEY TECHNOLOGIES

Radiocarbon dating, a test that allows archaeologists to date organic material, has helped researchers estimate the age of sites and other artifacts found at Stonehenge. Bone isotope testing on skeletons buried near Stonehenge has shown that people traveled great distances to visit the site.

IMPACT ON SCIENCE

The study of Stonehenge has proven that people living in Great Britain in prehistoric times were far better organized and more resourceful than archaeologists ever realized. The Riverside Project solved many of the mysteries that had surrounded Stonehenge since the Middle Ages and forever changed the way it will be studied in the future.

VISITING STONEHENGE

Stonehenge is one of Great Britain's most popular tourist attractions. Luckily, this makes it a relatively easy place to visit. Many tour companies offer bus trips that run from London to the stones. Travelers can also drive directly to the visitor's center in Wiltshire. From there, a ten-minute shuttle ride will take them to the stones. Visitors can walk around the site and take pictures. Stonehenge's busiest tourist time is July through September, when the weather is warmest. It is important to book tickets ahead of time to guarantee entry.

QUOTE

"In the past there was a tendency to look at these monumental landscapes and feel we understood them. But the more fieldwork we do, the more the story keeps changing."—*Julian Thomas, archaeologist and codirector of the Stonehenge Riverside Project*

GLOSSARY

antiquarian
A term mainly used in the 1600s through the 1800s to describe someone who studied ancient sites and collected relics from those places.

archaeoastronomy
The study of the astronomy of past cultures.

barracks
A building or group of buildings used to house soldiers.

barrow
A burial mound.

Briton
A member of the ancient peoples that inhabited Great Britain.

Bronze Age
The period of history lasting from approximately 2500 BCE to 1000 BCE in England.

Celt
A member of a group of people who inhabited ancient England and Western Europe.

Druid
A Celtic priest who lived in England from approximately 600 BCE to 60 CE.

excavation
An archaeological dig.

forensic
Relating to using science to solve crimes or legal problems.

lintel
The horizontal support across the top of a door or window. At Stonehenge, it refers to the horizontal stone laid across the top of uprights.

observatory
A place designed to observe natural objects and incidents, such as in astronomy.

Phoenician
A member of a group of people who lived near the Mediterranean Sea in southwest Asia in ancient times.

solstice
Either of the two times per year when the sun is at its greatest distance from the equator.

trilithon
The distinctive grouping of two upright stones with a lintel across the top found at Stonehenge.

ADDITIONAL RESOURCES

SELECTED BIBLIOGRAPHY

Atkinson, R. J. C. *Stonehenge*. New York: Penguin, 1990. Print.

Hawkins, Gerald S. *Stonehenge Decoded*. Garden City, NY: Doubleday, 1965. Print.

Hill, Rosemary. *Stonehenge*. Cambridge, MA: Harvard UP, 2008. Print.

Pearson, Mike Parker. *Stonehenge: A New Understanding*. New York: The Experiment, 2013. Print.

FURTHER READINGS

Allman, Toney. *Stonehenge*. San Diego: Referencepoint, 2008. Print.

Gray, Leon. *Solving the Mysteries of Stonehenge*. New York: Marshall Cavendish Benchmark, 2009. Print.

Henzel, Cynthia Kennedy. *Stonehenge*. Edina, MN: ABDO, 2011. Print.

WEBSITES

To learn more about Digging Up the Past, visit **booklinks.abdopublishing.com**. These links are routinely monitored and updated to provide the most current information available.

FOR MORE INFORMATION

For more information on this subject, contact or visit the following organizations:

AVEBURY

Marlborough, Wiltshire SN8 1RF, United Kingdom
+44 1672 539250
http://www.english-heritage.org.uk/daysout/properties/avebury
Built between approximately 2850 and 2200 BCE, Avebury is the largest stone circle in Great Britain. The Alexander Keiller Museum in the town of Avebury features many artifacts excavated in and around the circle.

STONEHENGE

Amesbury, Wiltshire SP4 7DE, United Kingdom
+44 870 333 1181
http://www.english-heritage.org.uk/daysout/properties/stonehenge
Visit this ancient site to see the stones firsthand. A center constructed in 2013 tells visitors the story of Stonehenge.

SOURCE NOTES

Chapter 1. If Stones Could Talk

1. Christopher Chippindale. *Stonehenge Complete*. New York: Thames and Hudson, 1994. Print. 10.

2. David Souden. *Stonehenge Revealed*. New York: Facts on File, 1997. Print. 12–13.

3. Ibid. 12–13.

4. "Stonehenge Construction." *Visit Stonehenge.com*. Visit Stonehenge.com, n.d. Web. 16 Nov. 2013.

5. Leon Stover. *Stonehenge City: A Reconstruction*. Jefferson, N.C.: McFarland, 2003. Print. 24–25.

6. Christopher Chippindale. *Stonehenge Complete*. New York: Thames and Hudson, 1994. Print. 15.

7. Ibid.

Chapter 2. The Antiquarians

1. "Research on Stonehenge," *English Heritage*. English Heritage, n.d. Web. 20 May 2013.

2. Geoffrey of Monmouth. *The History of the Kings of Britain*. Trans. Lewis Thorpe. Baltimore: Penguin, 1966. Print. 198.

3. "John Aubrey," *Encyclopedia of Archaeology: The Great Archaeologists*, Vol. 1. Ed. Tim Murray. Santa Barbara, CA: ABC-CLIO, 1999. Print. 18.

4. "Avebury." *English Heritage*. English Heritage, n.d. Web. 16 Nov. 2013.

5. "William Stukeley." *Encyclopedia of Archaeology: The Great Archaeologists*, Vol. 1. Ed. Tim Murray. Santa Barbara, CA: ABC-CLIO, 1999. Print. 40–41.

Chapter 3. Searching for a Pattern

1. Christopher Chippindale. *Stonehenge Complete*. New York: Thames and Hudson, 1994. Print. 113.

Chapter 4. The Victorians

1. Christopher Chippindale. *Stonehenge Complete*. New York: Thames and Hudson, 1994. Print. 128.
2. Ibid. 136–137.
3. Ibid.
4. Ibid. 137.

Chapter 5. Protecting the Stones

1. Christopher Chippindale. *Stonehenge Complete*. New York: Thames and Hudson, 1994. Print. 166.
2. Ibid. 172.

SOURCE NOTES CONTINUED

Chapter 6. More Discoveries

1. Rosemary Hill. *Stonehenge*. Cambridge, MA: Harvard U P, 2008. Print. 151–152.

2. Ibid. 152.

3. Christopher Chippindale. *Stonehenge Complete*. New York: Thames and Hudson, 1994. Print. 183.

4. Ibid.

5. "Stonehenge." *Britannia History*. Britannia.com, 2007. Web. 15 Nov. 2013.

6. Christopher Chippindale. *Stonehenge Complete*. New York: Thames and Hudson, 1994. Print. 187.

7. Tim Dowling. "The Non-Rolling Stone." *The Guardian*. Guardian News and Media, 7 Feb. 2003. Web. 15 Nov. 2013.

8. "Durrington Walls: Outer Ditch and Bank." *English Heritage*. English Heritage, n.d. Web. 15 Nov. 2013.

9. Trevor Rowley. *The English Landscape in the Twentieth Century*. New York: Hambledon Continuum, 2006. Print. x.

10. Christopher Chippindale. *Stonehenge Complete*. New York: Thames and Hudson, 1994. Print. 195.

Chapter 7. Stonehenge Decoded?

1. R. J. C. Atkinson. *Stonehenge*. New York: Penguin, 1990. Print. 144.

2. "Gerald Hawkins, 75, Stonehenge Scientist." *Boston Globe*. SunSentinel, 5 Aug. 2003. Web. 23 May 2013.

Chapter 8. Stonehenge for All

None.

Chapter 9. The Riverside Project

1. Mike Parker Pearson, et al. "The Stonehenge Riverside Project: Exploring the Neolithic Landscape of Stonehenge." *Documenta Praehistorica* XXXV (2008): 153–166. Web. 15 Nov. 2013.

2. Mike Parker Pearson. *Stonehenge: A New Understanding.* New York: The Experiment, 2013. Print. 92.

3. Ibid. 83.

4. Ibid. 177.

5. Ibid. 51.

6. Ibid. 312.

7. Eric A. Powell. "Bluestonehenge." *Archaeology* 63.1 (2010). *Archaeology Archive.* Archaeological Institute of America, 2009. Web. 15 Nov. 2013.

INDEX

age, 9, 22–23, 27, 29, 40–41, 48, 68–69
Air Corps, 56–57, 60
Altar Stone, 11, 55
Ambrosius, Aurelius, 14
Ancient Order of Druids, 48
antlers, 27, 45, 82, 96
Antrobus, Sir Edmund, 49
Antrobus family, 44–45, 48, 49
archaeoastronomy, 22, 72–74
artifacts, 28, 29, 53, 54, 62, 65, 82, 96
astronomical investigation, 39–41, 72–74
Atkinson, Richard, 58, 65, 67–72, 74, 78, 95
Aubrey, John, 16–18, 20, 23, 25, 53
Aubrey Holes, 9, 53, 62, 66, 83, 94
Avebury henge, 17, 18
Avenue, 9, 20, 39, 57, 69, 70, 89, 92, 93, 94
Avon, River, 8–9, 20, 57, 58, 70, 88–89, 91–93

Beanfield, Battle of, 78
Bluestonehenge, 92
bluestones, 10, 11, 35, 45, 53, 55–56, 58–59, 69, 70, 92, 94–95
bones, 15, 27, 28, 54, 66, 73, 78, 89, 90, 91, 97
Bronze Age, 31, 34, 37, 48, 67, 96
Burl, Aubrey, 56

Charlton, Walter, 16, 17
Chubb, Cecil, 49
Church of the Universal Bond, 48
construction, 7, 9, 11, 28, 38, 46–47, 53, 55–56
Crawford, O. G. S., 56–57
Cunnington, William, 26–29, 37, 53, 55

damage, 26–27, 44–45, 54, 95
Darwin, Charles, 33, 34
Druids, 18, 20, 21, 34, 38, 45, 48, 79
Duke of Buckingham, 15
Durrington Walls, 60, 73, 85, 86, 87, 88–89, 90, 92–93

English Heritage, 79–80, 81
Evans, Sir Arthur, 51, 78
excavations, 11, 15, 20, 27, 28, 29, 44, 45, 46, 52, 53–54, 62, 71

forensic investigation, 37

Geoffrey of Monmouth, 14
George V, 61–62
glaciers, 56
Gowland, William, 45, 46–47, 48, 52
guardians, 36

Hawkins, Gerald, 72–74
Hawley, William, 52–54, 62, 65
Heel Stone, 20, 39, 40, 72
Henry of Huntingdon, 13
Hoare, Colt, 28–29, 37

Iron Age, 31

James I, 15
Jones, Inigo, 15–16, 17
Judd, William, 36

ley lines, 61
Libby, Willard, 66
location, 8
Lockyer, Norman, 40, 41, 72
Lubbock, John, 36–37

magic, 14, 40
mathematical investigation, 38–41, 72, 74
Menter Preseli, 58
Merlin, 14, 40
moving stones, 14, 46–47, 56, 58–59, 71–72
Mycenae, 68

name meaning, 9
National Trust, 43, 62
Neolithic period, 11, 36–37, 46, 48, 67, 68
Newall, R. S., 53

orientation, 39

Paleolithic period, 36
Parker Pearson, Mike, 85–86, 87,
    88–89, 91–93, 94–96
Petrie, Flinders, 38–41, 44, 72
Piggott, Stuart, 65
preservation, 61, 63, 79
protection, 36, 43–44, 61, 79
Public Order Act, 79

radiocarbon dating, 66, 67–68, 72,
    82, 83, 92, 93
Ramilisonina, 85–86, 93
restoration, 43, 45, 51, 62, 69

Salisbury Plain, 8, 14, 27, 35, 37, 48,
    55, 56, 57, 59, 62, 68
sarsen stones, 10, 26, 34, 35, 44,
    45, 53, 54–55, 67, 69, 70, 94, 95
skeletons, 37
Slaughter Stone, 11, 28, 53, 94
sound qualities, 52
Station Stones, 83
Stone, J. F. S., 65
Stone Age, 31, 36–37, 59, 73, 90
Stonehenge Archer, The, 78
Stonehenge Decoded, 72, 73
Stonehenge Free Festival, 77
stones falling, 11, 26–27, 44–45, 69
Stukeley, William, 18, 20, 21, 22–23,
    25, 34, 38–39, 57, 72
summer solstice, 35, 39, 48, 63,
    77–78, 79–81, 90

theories about use, 11, 13–14, 16,
    18–20, 22, 34, 38–40, 56, 61,
    73–74, 86, 92–93
Thomas, H. H., 54–56
Thomsen, Christian, 29, 31, 34
Thurnam, John, 37
tourism, 35, 36, 40, 43, 44, 63, 80
trilithons, 10–11, 26, 44, 52, 69, 94

UFO sightings, 61
United Nations Educational,
    Science and Cultural
    Organization, 79

Wainwright, Geoffrey, 73, 88
Watkins, Albert, 61
Wilson, Sir Daniel, 37
Wiltshire, 8, 16, 28, 49, 52, 54, 78
World War I, 48–49, 51, 60
worship, 11, 48, 79

ABOUT THE AUTHOR

Michael Capek is a former teacher who lives with his family in Covington, Kentucky. He has been in love with archaeology since he was boy, finding arrowheads in the fields and streams near his home in rural northern Kentucky. Capek is the author of award-winning books for young readers, most of them about history.

DATE I